MARKED BY PRAYER

I0806045

FIVE TRAITS OF PEOPLE WHO PRAY

MARKED BY PRAYER

G. DWAYNE McCRARY

B&H
PUBLISHING®
BRENTWOOD, TENNESSEE

979-8-3845-3425-9

Published by B&H Publishing Group
Brentwood, Tennessee

Dewey Decimal Classification: 248.3
Subject Heading: PRAYER / CHRISTIAN LIFE / DISCIPLESHIP

Cover design and illustrations by Lindy Kasler.
Author photo by Lifeway Staff.

1 2 3 4 5 6 • 29 28 27 26

Dedicated to my monthly prayer partners, thank you for showing me what it looks like to be marked by prayer.

CONTENTS

Introduction

WE ARE MARKED!

No matter how hard we may try, we continue to be detected. It may be our accent, our clothing, or how we mingle (or don't). No matter how hard we try, we are detected by the locals who somehow know. We are marked.

We can watch our diet, exercise, and do everything our doctors tell us, and still deal with heart disease. Some things are simply in our DNA. We are marked by genetics.

Soldiers may be thousands of miles from a battlefield, but those experiences feel like the battle is next door. We may never have been a soldier but still carry marks from other experiences that cause us to respond to items that trigger a memory. We are marked by our experiences.

People judge us by the schools we attended, expecting us to carry a certain attitude based on their view of others they know who attended that school. The same is true of our employers, past and present. We are marked by relationships.

Some marks can be emotional, psychological, and physical. I broke my leg playing football in high school, and that experience involved all three of these. Physical scars decorate both sides of my right ankle. Seeing a player injured brings back the emotions of that day and the psychological triggers that surround it. I am marked.

Marks can also carry spiritual significance. The scars on my ankle remind me that God used that broken leg to draw me to Himself. Staring at the cast made me ask some honest questions that were only answerable by Him.

Followers of Jesus are told by Paul that we are to display the fruit of the Spirit. We are to show "love, joy, peace, patience, kindness, goodness, faithfulness, gentleness, and self-control" (Gal. 5:22–23). In this same letter, Paul also declared that he carried "the marks of Jesus" in his body (Gal. 6:17). Paul was talking about the physical scars from the beatings, chains, riots, and host of other indignities experienced because of his commitment to Christ (see 2 Cor. 6:3–10).

Jesus told His disciples that they should expect to be marked both physically and spiritually. Peter was told that he would be led to a place where he did not want to go with his hands stretched out (John 21:18–19). Jesus warned His disciples that they would be treated the same way He had been treated (John 15:20). He died on a cross, and they were to expect the same kind of mistreatment and ridicule simply because they were associated with Him. Jesus also reminded His disciples that they would demonstrate love to such a degree that they would become known for that love (John 13:35). John echoed this teaching, as he called for his readers to lay down their lives for others, just as Jesus had done for us (1 John 3:16–18). Benson in his commentary on John 13:35 identifies this love that is to be shown as the "noblest badge of our profession."[1] When we see the word *badge*, we should think "marked."

Love is the fruit of the Spirit that shows our commitment to Jesus. So, how does prayer fit into this? Prayer is not listed as a fruit of the Spirit. However, prayer is part of the pathway that enables us to demonstrate the fruit listed. The fruit comes from an abiding relationship with the Father and grows through that relationship. Prayer enters the picture at this point since our relationship with the Father grows through our dialoguing with Him. We learn His heart and are then able to respond in a way that reflects His heart. We are to be marked by prayer.

How Did I Get Here?

Like many of you, I am a fellow learner when it comes to prayer. Prayer was modeled by the church in which I grew up and by some key leaders who impacted me through their prayer life. These leaders sought out people to ask them about their life and then prayed for that person. I was a benefactor of their commitment to prayer. Notes received are treated as priceless treasures and are evidence of their being marked by prayer. I don't count myself in that group. I wish that were not the case, but I am a novice when compared to them. No one is more surprised about my writing this book than I am.

This book began with a group of people sitting around a table discussing how we can encourage church leaders to lead their churches to pray more effectively. During that conversation, one member of that circle began praying, directing a prayer for me to be a champion for prayer. As he prayed, terror filled me with that thought. That is not me. Teacher, sure. Organizer and planner, you bet. Conference leader, bring it on. Champion of prayer . . . NOPE.

As that prayer time concluded, the people sitting around that table shared favorite books about prayer. Once I got home, the most referenced books were added to my reading list. I gleaned prayer practices and tips through that reading and added more books to the reading list. In the process of reading, patterns began to emerge that pointed to characteristics possessed by people known for their prayer life. These characteristics were more than practices; they were marks. They were marked by prayer.

Those patterns then led to an examination of Scripture. My quest was to determine if these same marks could be seen in a Bible character. Doing so was a challenge since we mostly see only snapshots of their lives. John even tells us as much in his Gospel account (John 21:25). However, several Bible characters were identified with clues about how they were marked. In effect, they give us actions we can take to foster that marking in our own lives.

In the pages that follow, we will examine five markings that emerged through my reading and reflection. People of prayer:

1. Experienced helplessness in some way
2. Voice prayers informed by Scripture
3. Exhibit personal grief over sin
4. Possess a deferred confidence
5. Are consumed with God's presence

We will focus on these five markings, dedicating a chapter to each. We will explore a snapshot from the life of a Bible personality who demonstrates that marking and propose some actions we can take that put us in a position to be marked as well.

During this season, God taught me some important things about people marked by prayer. As already shared, this journey included the reading of several books on prayer. (I still have a few more to read on my list.) I wanted to simply read their stories and learn from them, thinking that the knowledge gained would be enough. But God tends to let us experience the truth so we understand the nuances of that truth.

Gaining knowledge is important, but it's not nearly as important as the practice. We tend to want knowledge and not the experience. Experience carries a price tag, and that would be true for the marks of prayer. Marks are not cheap or easy.

As you read this book and other books on prayer, my hope is that God will mark you with these same traits. This prayer is a hard and dangerous request especially when considering the nature of these traits. The path to being marked is not easy. While transforming and painful, this quest for the marks is worth the transparency and effort.

Chapter 1

HELPLESS

People marked by prayer experienced helplessness in some way.

We purchased a new electric can opener. My wife had no trouble whatsoever with the new kitchen gadget. The hum could be heard from another room as she opened a can. Then it was my turn to use it. I have no idea what I was doing wrong, but the gadget never locked on the can I wanted to open. Nothing worked, and my wife was not home at the time to help me.

In desperation, I began to look for the instructions, but they were nowhere to be found. Later, the instructions were discovered sitting on the kitchen table. I had been too frustrated to notice. The old electric can opener had already been thrown away so that was not an option either. Eventually, a manual can opener was located in a drawer under some serving spoons, and I was happy to use that tool to get the can opened.

Not being able to get that new can opener to work brought in a sense of helplessness, especially since I knew my wife had used it just hours before without any problem. The potential of finding the manual opener gave me hope as the useless electric can opener sat on the counter mocking me. That opener would mock me again after my wife returned and placed it on a can and it worked without a hitch, making me feel even more helpless than before.

Plenty of other things in life can make us feel helpless. A flat tire in the middle of rush hour while it's raining. Being given a task to complete by our boss that no one else has been able to figure out. Looking at our bank account and knowing there is more month to cover than there is money in the bank. Approaching storms, relationships, injustices, and a variety of other items could be added to this list. The point is we have all faced things in life that leave us feeling helpless. If this has not happened to you yet, get ready. It will.

When we look at the lives of people who are marked by prayer, we tend to find a defining life event that made them feel helpless. This event can be a cancer diagnosis for themselves or a spouse, a child born with a disability, a prodigal child, or a work challenge. Most of these events relate to someone they love or trust with that event testing that love and trust.

Since we all face situations that cause us to feel helpless, the issue is more about how we respond to the event rather than about the event itself. Two people can face the same challenge, both feeling helpless, but one feeling hopeless while the other is filled with hope.

Helpless is defined as "being unable to defend ourselves or unable to act without help." No matter how much I tried, the new electric can opener was not cooperating. Nothing I did worked. However, hope was found in knowing that help was available, immediately in the manual can opener and ultimately in my wife's sharing her expertise. Hope came through being able to search and ask. Had I not been able to search or ask, the helplessness would have morphed into hopelessness.

People marked with helplessness understand that hopelessness can be avoided. They live with the realization that God can always be found, and as long as He is present, there is hope. David gives us a picture of what this helplessness looks like.

Helpless King David

David dug himself into a helpless situation. He had faced many challenges in his lifetime including a giant and a father-in-law who was out to get him. He had fought many battles, and now his troops were fighting yet another one. Instead of being in the field, we find him staying behind in one of his palaces. He spied the spouse of one of his elite warriors bathing. David would have known she was married since she was introduced to him as the wife of Uriah. He summoned her and they committed adultery. Bathsheba discovered she was pregnant, and since her husband was deployed, David was obviously the father of the child. David arranged for Uriah the mighty warrior to get some leave, thinking he would spend that time with Bathsheba so the child would appear to be his. That did not happen, and Uriah was sent back to the front lines with a sealed letter. True to the directions in the letter, Joab sent Uriah into the fiercest part of the battle where he was killed (see 2 Sam. 11).

Thinking he had covered all his tracks, David then took Bathsheba as his wife. Enter Nathan who confronted David about his adultery and murder conspiracy. In 2 Samuel 12, we are told that David would be forgiven, but the child yet to be born would not survive. After birth the infant became ill, so David fasted. After seven days the child died. Imagine those seven days as David prayed and fasted, knowing that the child was ill because of his own sin. David was helpless at that point. He could do nothing to change the situation or hide from his sin.

Out of that helplessness David turned to God. Where else could he turn? No other help was available. He was king, but the crown on his head and accolades received were useless now. Most would view David as a resourceful and capable person, able to get himself out of some tight situations. He even played like he had gone mad and was able to escape from the hands of Achish (see 1 Sam. 21:12–15). No escapes were present for David to get himself out of the mess he had created.

Out of that season of helplessness, David wrote Psalms 32 and 51, two of the more read and studied psalms. Both psalms point to our need for help when it comes to our sin (more on this in chapter 3). We are not sure how many of the other psalms came out of this experience, but we know these two did at least and can imagine that this experience profoundly impacted how David dialogued with God moving forward.

Other Bible personalities experienced helplessness: King Hezekiah in Isaiah 38, the Canaanite woman in Matthew 15, Peter while imprisoned in Acts 12, and Paul and Silas while in prison in Philippi in Acts 16. In and of their own power, no actions would change their situation. They needed help and found it in the only

One who could help. That helplessness drove them to trust God. They were not hopeless but helpless, unable to find a resolution in and of themselves.

When We Are Helpless

When we read about the experiences of people marked by prayer, we eventually find them sharing about a time in which they felt helpless and embraced it.

Those helpless moments make us useful vessels for God's purposes. We do not fully understand the power and promise of prayer until after we become helpless because that helplessness pushes us to fully depend on God. Helplessness also invites us to seek His heart and not ours. In those helpless moments we learn to follow Him, staying in step as He leads, and we learn that our hearts can and will deceive us. Once we align with His heart, we find contentment.

This alignment begins with accepting that we are helpless. Salvation is the ultimate expression of helplessness as we come to Christ acknowledging our inability to rescue ourselves. But salvation is just a first step. As we face other challenges, we find ourselves needing to accept that we are helpless once again. Freedom is found in embracing our helplessness because we are turning to the One who is able to provide the needed aid. We grow in our trust of God as a result, which is manifest in our prayers.

Wait and Seek

Jeremiah faithfully delivered God's message for more than forty years and was mostly ignored. God told him that would be the case, but knowing this did not make being ignored any easier. In Lamentations we find a man who had witnessed the destruction he had foretold. Jerusalem was in ruins and God's people were in exile, away from their promised land. In the middle of his lament, Jeremiah gives us two actions to take when feeling helpless. In Lamentations 3:25, we are told to wait and seek.

We see these two actions in David's life as well after the birth of the first child with Bathsheba. Waiting and seeking were his only options.

Waiting is not my strength. That would be the understatement of this book! Many of us are wired with a drive to get something fixed when it breaks so we can keep moving forward, checking boxes on our to-do lists. Most of us do not include a line on our to-do list for waiting. And yet Jeremiah included it as an action to take when we find ourselves in a helpless position, and it was what David did as well.

Waiting makes sense when we are helpless since action may very well make the situation worse. Waiting requires us to get out of the way and let God do what only He can do. Our tendency is to try to do what only God can do, something we are not qualified to attempt. Waiting is an admission that we are helpless and in need of God. We may wonder with King David how long we need to wait for God to act (see Ps. 13); however, doing so does not negate our need to wait.

A related challenge is admitting we are helpless. Jeremiah could preach all day long, but he could not make the people respond to his message. David could call on all the doctors and prophets available to him, and the child would still die. The sooner we realize we are helpless, the better.

Waiting does not mean sitting. Think about the role of a waiter in your favorite restaurant. We rarely see them sitting. The term *waiter* has its origin with attendants of nobility standing at the ready in the dining room waiting to serve, ensuring that the needs of the people eating were met. When we wait on God, we don't sit back and coast. Instead, we serve. We serve those who are hurting, those who are encouraging us, and those whom God places in our path during that season.

The second action recommended by Jeremiah was seeking. David took this same action. In Psalm 32:5–7, David declares that he acknowledged his sin to God, seeking Him while God could be found. This declaration emphasizes David seeking God. We are promised that if we seek Him, we will find Him. But what does that seeking look like? Is it more than calling out to Him or going to a worship service? Jeremiah reminded the Israelites who were in exile that they would seek after God and find Him and added that they were to search for God with all their heart (Jer. 29:13). This passage also promised their restoration as God's people, which reminds us of why they were banished from the promised land in the first place.

Their sin was simple; they had abandoned God as their only love. They still wanted God's blessings but not the relationship that came with those blessings.

They would remain in exile for seventy years, which required them to keep seeking. Plenty of opportunities would exist in those seventy years to stop seeking. Many would never see Jerusalem again, but that was not to be an excuse for discontinuing the seeking. Even in exile, they could ask God to show them what He wanted them to know about Him. He had not ceased being God, nor could He only be God if they were in Jerusalem or the temple. Being in exile gave them an opportunity to learn that God was capable of sustaining them even in Babylon. God would use that time to help His people regain their focus on Him, but they had to seek Him in a foreign land for them to rediscover Him.

The same is true for us. We too must keep seeking as we wait. Jeremiah combined these two actions on purpose. God's discipline and redemptive plans called for them (and us) to wait. Their need demanded that they seek as they waited. Both were necessary then and are necessary now. Together, they foster trust in God at all times and develop the habit of turning to God first when facing life's challenges.

It helps when we have people in our friendship circle who turn to God first as a regular habit and will hold us accountable to do the same, but someone has to set the standard. God was inviting His people to set that standard by waiting and seeking, knowing that doing so would be the first step in their being marked as His and by a trust in Him seen in every area of their lives, including prayer.

Your Turn

List things going on in your life that make you feel helpless. Pray about these items, using Psalm 13 as a guide.

Taking a Deeper Look

Review Psalms 51 and 32, looking for expressions that point to helplessness and hopefulness.

Compare the stories of King Hezekiah in Isaiah 38, the Canaanite woman in Matthew 15, Peter while imprisoned in Acts 12, and Paul and Silas while in prison in Philippi in Acts 16. How did their helplessness drive them to God?

Use a concordance to look at passages in the Bible that include the words *wait* and *seek*, especially passages that include both words. What do you learn about these two actions? How are they related? What are you waiting for? How can you seek God while waiting?

Chapter 2

SCRIPTURE IS CENTRAL

People marked by prayer voice prayers informed by Scripture.

Some movie lines become so ingrained they define a culture and ethos for a generation. The ones we recognize immediately reveal our age and the tribe to which we belong. Those lines are how we connect within our tribe. We don't need to explain the scene or the impact of the line, we simply need to say the line, and everything around that scene suddenly appears in the minds of the people in our tribe. If we quote part of the line, members of our tribe may add the rest of it automatically. Even when we misuse or incorrectly state the quote, members of the tribe may correct us so that we are true to the movie and what that line represents.

If we were each to list our most memorable movie lines, we would see a characteristic we admire or aspire to possess. We either identify with the character or wish we were that character. We want to run the steps of the Philadelphia Museum of Art, have the confidence to capture a large shark, or display an adventurous spirit that takes us to remote places in pursuit of an archeological treasure.

The memorable line may tell us something about the plot of the movie. In some cases, a single memorable line helps us remember the moral or main message of the movie. These memorable lines are how the movie keeps speaking to us even when we are not sitting in the theater.

So, what does all this have to do with the Bible? The Bible defines our tribe. In it we discover our Creator who loves us and created us with purpose. We failed Him, and He is now working to redeem His creation. That redemption takes place through faith in His resurrected Son who is also fully God and fully human. This world is moving toward a day when the redemption secured through Jesus will be fully realized in what the Old Testament calls the Day of the Lord.

When we hear a key phrase from Scripture—"In the beginning," "For God so loved," "In my Father's house," "I am"—we are reminded of the character of God. We gain a glimpse of what it means to be His people and how we should conduct our lives in light of being His people. We may be able to finish the rest of the statement and recall the scene and context surrounding that statement. Just as some value the lines in a movie, we should value the statements we find in Scripture.

People marked by prayer demonstrate the value of Scripture through their prayers. They may spend more time examining and reflecting on the Bible than they do in what one might call the actual practice of prayer. The intent of the study is to understand

God's will and heart, which we see in the patterns found in Scripture. In *The Doctrine of Prayer*, T. W. Hunt explains how prayer when coupled with Bible study enables us to understand God's heart and mind, so we can then properly carry out God's rule in His creation. Dr. Hunt emphasized that the purpose of prayer was all about accomplishing God's will.[2] Knowing what God thinks and how He thinks enables us to rule as assigned to us in Genesis 1 within His character and will, as if He was the one ruling.

For the person marked by prayer, biblically informed prayer, is more than a device to bring variety to prayer. Scripture keeps their prayers from going into the ditch of selfishness, pride, and sin. Left to ourselves, our prayer life could easily reflect our wants and desires to the exclusion of God's wants and desires. Responding to Scripture in our prayer time moves us to a "Thy will be done" attitude that keeps in check our "my will be done" tendencies, the same "Thy will be done" attitude we see in Jesus when praying in the garden hours before He would hang on a cross (Luke 22:42). His words on the cross give us a glimpse of how Scripture informed Jesus's prayer life.

Jesus—Praying on the Cross

Betrayed, beaten, mocked, and attached to a tree, we find Jesus entering the final hours of that most painful of days. He has asked the Father to forgive those casting lots for His clothing, assured the thief of a place in heaven, and directed John to care for Mary. When the sun should have been at its height, darkness descended on the earth at noon. Jesus said nothing for three hours (see Matt.

27:45–56) as He endured being suspended above the earth as it sat in an eerie darkness. Many have wondered what Jesus thought during those three hours. Was He reviewing the sins of you and I as He bore them on that tree? Did He think about people who had abandoned Him on this day? We may have a clue as to His thoughts by what Jesus declared as the darkness began to subside; He quoted Psalm 22:1, "My God, my God, why have you abandoned me?" He had endured the insults and shaking of heads told about in Psalm 22:7. He heard the taunts to deliver Himself as declared in Psalm 22:8, and He had watched the dividing of His clothes foretold in Psalm 22:18. These took place prior to noon and the darkness.

In this most poignant moment in history, we see Jesus quoting a psalm, showing us the role Scripture should play as He quoted a lament psalm helping Him express the emotion of that horrible moment and helping us interpret what was going on. As ugly as the first eighteen verses of Psalm 22 read, the second half is filled with hope and victory. This psalm serves as a summary of the finished work of Jesus as He secured our atonement. The psalm ends with a declaration that the work of righteousness had been done, or finished, like the final words of Jesus on the cross.

In Psalm 22, we find David lamenting God's absence for a season but remaining confident in God's answering nonetheless. That confidence is tempered with humility as the psalmist declared himself to be a worm with no reputation. We don't know what was going on in David's life that led to the writing of this psalm. References are made in the psalm that point to crucifixion, but that cruel form of execution was unknown to David, not even existing until hundreds of years after his lifetime. As a result, some scholars see this psalm as pure prophecy. In Peter's sermon on the day of Pentecost found in Acts 2, he called David a prophet who foresaw the future death and resurrection of the Messiah (vv. 29–33).

However, this psalm became part of the Jewish celebration of Purim, commemorating the deliverance of the Hebrews from the hands of Haman by Esther's intervention. They faced complete annihilation, yet God used Esther to negate the threat. With this psalm being used in connection with Purim, the Jewish interpretation would hold that David and the Hebrews would be the ones referenced in this psalm. Some Jewish scholars identify David's being in anguish after being betrayed by some of his family and former friends as he fled the rebellion identified in 2 Samuel 16. If that is the case, then David was in a dark place as he penned these words. It really does not need to be an either-or. God could have used an experience of David as a backdrop for writing these words, knowing that these words would see their ultimate fulfillment as Jesus hung on the tree.

While the words of Jesus were heard by those near the cross, He directed some of what He said on the cross to the Father. In short, He was praying and allowing us to eavesdrop. In the darkest and most challenging moment of His life, we find Jesus praying with Scripture at the forefront, with Psalms 22 and 31 being the focus. The words spoken by Jesus in the afternoon, the final four recorded quotes—"Why have you forsaken me?" "I thirst," "It is finished," and "Into your hands I commend my Spirit"—can all be found in the psalms.

Jesus's final cry uttered from the cross was a quote from Psalm 31. The psalm is a statement of trust in God regardless of the challenges one may face. The psalm ends with a declaration of praise for God's goodness and kindness. Interestingly, this psalm is alluded to by Stephen as he was stoned (Acts 7:59). Even more interesting is Paul quoting from this psalm when encouraging the Corinthians in his first letter (1 Cor. 16:3; see Ps. 31:24). Remember Paul was a witness to Stephen's execution.

In Scripture we find the words that escape us when we need them the most. Our human limits and emotions get in the way of our clearly articulating what is going on inside. We may have so much going on inside we cannot sort it all out. Scripture gives us a means to do so. As we memorize and recall passages, we connect with the God who directed the writing of those words in the first place. That connecting with God is what gives the clarity we so desperately need. This clarity comes through letting Scripture inform our prayers, following the practice of Jesus as seen on the cross.

Developing the Practice

Stories abound of people who opened the Bible and prayed what they read void of study and context. Some are shared in jest, and others are shared to illustrate the problem with misusing Scripture. The Holy Spirit can direct us as we search for a Bible passage for the day or sort through notices received on our phones with a daily verse suggestion. But He can also use the discipline of Bible study to direct our prayers as we discover cross references, key words, and critical doctrines that add depth not only to what we pray and how we pray but also to our understanding of the God to whom we pray and of His heart's desires for His creation.

Jesus knew the meaning behind Psalm 22 and the context. He did not misapply the psalm to His situation, knowing exactly how to handle the truth or cut it as Paul might say (2 Tim. 2:15). Granted, comparing ourselves to Jesus when it comes to understanding the Bible creates some challenges. God inspired men to write the words we find in Scripture, which gives Jesus an advantage we don't have. However, we cannot forget that Jesus was human and spent the time needed to understand these words from a human perspective. We must depend on the Holy Spirit to direct us at this point, knowing that He gives us what we need when we need it.

Depending on the Holy Spirit does not negate our need to let Bible study inform our prayer time. Notice the use of the word *study* and not *reading*. Differences abound between the two. We can read something without studying it, but we cannot study without reading it. When asked if we read a chapter in a book, we can indicate that we have and mean a variety of things from viewing the headings of each section to doing a deep dive by fact-checking the content. However, if we are asked if we studied a chapter, the expectation is that we have given some deliberate thought to the content and sought to gain a clear understanding of the subject matter. The goal is different.

Prayers should come out of our studying Scripture and not merely our reading a few verses looking for something that affirms our desires in some way. If we separate prayer from Bible study, we run the risk of praying out of ignorance. We may still pray out of ignorance since our understanding may be limited, but we will be less likely to pray without the heart of God in mind. Scripture serves as a guardrail in life, and that includes our prayer life. We are not worshiping the Bible in doing so but rather the God who speaks to us through His Bible.

Presenting a comprehensive section on how to study and interpret the Bible is beyond the scope of this book. However, we would be negligent if we failed to give some direction here.

Olin Binkley gave some general guidelines in his book *How to Study the Bible*. In the section on examining words and historical settings, he identities these actions:

> - Seek diligently to understand what each biblical writer meant by the words and phrases he used.
> - Interpret the words of a biblical text in their context.
> - Learn as much as possible about the historical situation in which each book of the Bible was written.[3]

These assume that we are interested in doing more than simply reading the Bible and are driven to understand the Bible as a whole work.

Group Involvement

One action that can help us is to get involved in a group that regularly studies the Bible together. In his journal from 1919, Arthur

Flake connected personal Bible study with group study. He observed that people who are involved in a weekly Bible study group were much more likely to study the Bible for themselves than those who were not involved in a group.[4] The observation makes sense since a group holds us accountable and motivates us to study so we can participate more fully in the group, and doing so encourages us to engage in deeper reflection afterward.

We are talking here about groups that focus on actually studying the Bible. They may use a resource like the ones created by Lifeway to guide their study and keep them out of the ditches, but the Bible text is the central focus. Groups can exist where the focus is more on topics beyond Bible study, and we want to be clear about what kind of group we are highlighting here.

Schedule Some Individual Study Time

A second step is to set aside daily time to study the Bible. This is where resources like the ones mentioned above from Lifeway can help. Following a study guide makes it a little easier and usually helps us develop our Bible study skills along the way. Cross-references, word studies, map skills, connecting locations, and other Bible skills serve as a backbone for many of these guides, which help us learn to do many of these study skills. We may have other items we consult including a study Bible, commentary, atlas, Bible dictionary or handbook, and concordance, which add to what we find in a provided study guide. Personal study gives us the time we need to reflect and consider the intricacies of a Bible passage, while group study motivates us and gives us a place to double-check our findings and conclusions. We need both individual and group study.

Connect What We Are Studying with Our Prayer Life

Books abound with plans for praying. Some plans are built around acrostics, and others are built around the prayer found in Matthew 6 (commonly called the Lord's Prayer). Instead of examining the merits and challenges of each approach, let's look at a simple and hopefully practical way of connecting our Bible study time with prayer. This came out of a conversation with my son. We were talking about some of the things I was learning through my reading that included some of the models suggested by different writers. As we talked, we began to realize that we both needed a simple framework. We needed some type of structure, beyond the "let the Spirit lead" and short of using a prescriptive pattern like Adoration, Confession, Thanksgiving, and Supplication (ACTS model)[5] or a formula based on Matthew 6. As we talked, we realized how much we can complicate things. We needed something we could do that was easy and adaptable, something for the rest of us who need to start simple. We landed on two questions that gave us focus on how Scripture should inform our prayer. These two questions are:

> How does God reveal Himself in this passage?
>
> How should we respond to what He reveals?

Conversations work that way. One person talks, revealing to the other what they want them to know, and then the other person responds to what was revealed. If they responded in a way that showed no connection to what the first person said, we would wonder if the second person was even listening. The expectation of a conversation is that the person responds to what was just said, and prayer should be no different.

Some coworkers helped craft a set of prayer prompts for Psalm 148 based on these two questions. Psalm 148 portrays all of creation as praising God in which there is a progression from the first items that existed (the heavens and heights) to humanity and ends with God raising a horn for His people. God is the strength in the psalm with Jesus being the ultimate expression of that strength and protection (see Luke 1:69).

Here are the prompts we created following the Two Questions approach:

> Read Psalm 148, noticing how the progression points to God's creating with purpose. Thank Him for being a God of purpose and commit to follow His purposes in your life this week.
>
> Read Psalm 148, noticing how every aspect of God's creation should praise their Creator. Pray to the Lord, joining in this praise of our God for His good creation and faithful provision and care, and pray for boldness to call others to come close to Jesus by faith.
>
> Read Psalm 148, focusing on the horn of salvation in verse 14. Thank God for providing salvation through His Son, the horn of salvation, and ask God to help you invite one person to turn to Jesus as your act of praise this week.

Other passages were being studied, so we sought to create prayer prompts that followed this same framework for something other than a psalm. In Revelation 12:11, God is revealed as the sacrificed Lamb who provides salvation, the One faithful to His people (Ps. 34:8) and worthy of devotion. Jesus demonstrates this same type of devotion in the garden prayer found in Mark 14:36. In response to how God is revealed, we admit that we need Him, accepting His provision for our salvation, and praise Him for freeing us. We concluded the prayer with a commitment to share with others about His goodness as we go through this day and expressing our need for His help today to place His will ahead of our own, following Jesus throughout the day.

Acts 1:24 was a second passage we considered. The early church leaders were trying to decide who should take the chair that had been vacated by Judas Iscariot. They made a simple request, stating, "You, Lord, know everyone's hearts; show which of these two you have chosen." What we find out about God here is He knows everything including our hearts and He also has plans for each of us. There was a plan for Barsabbas and Matthias. Here is one way we could express a prayer based on Acts 1:24:

> God, I am grateful that you know me better than I know myself. Since You know my heart, God, help me know my heart like You do. Show me the things that keep me from being all You created me to be. I know You have a plan for me, so help me take a step today to fulfill that plan. I am

> available to do whatever You desire, trusting that You will show others along the way what those desires are so I can do the tasks You place before me with confidence in You and You alone.

Many define prayer as a conversation between us and God. The problem is we tend to forget that conversations are two-way, with one person taking the lead. Our tendency is to take the lead in our prayer conversations, limiting ourselves to what God may show us and direct us to do. When Scripture becomes our starting point, we are inviting God to take the lead in the conversation so we can then respond to His words with a view to carrying out His will in His creation.

Keeping a prayer journal took on a new dimension. The journal was no longer a list of actions for God to take but rather a recording of what God said and my response to what He said. Including a list of needs got in the way of seeing what God was saying and wanted me to do in response. Instead of approaching God with an agenda, this approach opened me to God's agenda for my day.

Your Turn

Review the passage examined by the Bible study group you most recently attended. Record your response to the two questions:

> How does God reveal Himself in this passage?
>
> How do I respond to how God reveals Himself?

Record a prayer based on how you answered these two questions.

Create a journal for recording your prayers. Select a Bible book, and let that book drive your prayer focus, reading digestible sections each morning. Record the date, the passage reviewed, what God revealed, and how you responded.

Taking a Deeper Look

Read Psalm 22 and the events recorded in the Gospels on the day of Jesus's crucifixion (Matt. 27; Mark 15; Luke 23; John 19). Analyze the psalm as a prayer, looking for themes and how God is revealed in the psalm. How are those themes and God's revealing of Himself also seen in the work done through Jesus and the cross?

Chapter 3

PERSONAL GRIEF

People marked by prayer exhibit personal grief over sin.

The second week of a new semester included a meeting with one of the faculty. We met around a portable TV he had tucked into a corner of his office so we could witness history although remotely. The sound was just high enough for us to listen while having the discussion we were supposed to have as student and advisor. The date was January 28, 1986, and our conversation took a back seat as the countdown began. We watched in amazement as the *Challenger* began to lift off the pad. That amazement turned to dismay as we watched the rest of that ill-fated takeoff.

As the commentators explained the scene, the professor began to weep and to mumble. His mumblings were unclear, but you could tell he was praying.

Then there was me. My thoughts were dominated with how this event would impact the Bible study I would be leading the next evening. I tried to be as grieved as the professor, but it was not happening. Thoughts about what was wrong with me began to swirl in my head. Why was I not as moved emotionally as he? Was I just calloused and uncaring? What will the professor think of me if he looks over and sees me tearless?

Eventually, the professor gathered himself, and we headed to our respective classes. This was personal to him, and he owned the grief of that moment. He was thinking about everyone impacted, while I was thinking about me. We both saw the exact same thing, and yet we had vastly different reactions for a variety of reasons.

The same is true of sin. Two people can get caught in the exact same act and yet respond differently. One person can take full responsibility, even regretting that they influenced another person to participate, while the other is more than happy to pass on the blame to anyone they can think of as long as doing so gets them off the hook. We have all been there, looking for a way to escape.

We stated earlier in this book that one goal of prayer is to understand God's heart. The Bible is clear that God loves His creation. Peter wrote in his second letter that God wants all people to come to repentance (2 Pet. 3:9). The problem is on our end and our unwillingness to repent from our sin through placing our faith in Jesus. It is on our back and not His.

We are a rebellious group and have been for a long time. In Genesis 6 we find humanity becoming proficient in wickedness. We mastered it and committed our mental powers to finding new ways of demonstrating evil. We were so proficient that God regretted creating us. We showed little of the One in whose image we were created. The majority is not always right.

Moses, the writer of Genesis, tells us that God "was deeply grieved" over our sin (Gen. 6:6). Let's compare how different translations treat the last phrase in verse 6.

CSB: "He was deeply grieved."

KJV: "It grieved him at his heart."

NASB: "He was grieved in His heart."

NIV: "His heart was deeply troubled."

NLT: "It broke his heart."

NET: "He was highly offended."

Another way of understanding this phrase in Genesis 6:6 is that God was pained or pierced. Can we truly understand the hurt sin causes God? Our sin, as individuals and as a whole, cuts the heart of God causing Him to grieve deeply, and people marked by prayer carry that same grief. They also understand that God's grief over our sin does not negate His love.

We may struggle with God's sending a flood to wipe out the world and yet still loving us even when the Bible clearly tells us that God is love. We can forget that forgiveness and repentance are a package deal. We do not find the people in Noah's day seeking God or His forgiveness. Instead, we find them looking for new ways of defying Him as they watched Noah build an ark. Paul reminded the Romans that all of us are accountable for our actions, knowing right from wrong in some way and yet choosing to do wrong. Our sin is the problem, and our sin breaks God's heart.

Most of us will go to great lengths to keep from reflecting on our sin. We see this subtlety in how we approach Easter. If we could pick, we would rather talk about Sunday, the resurrection, and Jesus defeating death, and not talk about what happened on Friday. The cross is an ugly reminder of our sin. Isaiah reminds us that Jesus would be crushed because of *our* iniquity, *our* sin. He would be bruised, battered, and beaten beyond recognition because of *our* sin. We need the Friday of Easter just as much as we need Sunday. The importance of reflecting on our sin is seen in the Lord's Supper. This observance instituted by Jesus points to His death, the broken bread and the spilled blood, and not His resurrection. We need Good Friday if we are going to grieve over our sin.

For the person marked by prayer, Good Friday is just as welcomed as resurrection Sunday. They understand God's heart, where grief over sin and love for humanity are wrapped into a single act. The person marked by prayer understands that grief over sin is a function of love. Love for others is what drives the grief. Because they love the people trapped by sin, they grieve for them, knowing God has something better.

We looked at two responses to the *Challenger*'s failed liftoff, and now we look at the reaction of two people who were confronted about their sin. One made excuses while the other acted, demonstrating grief.

Abraham and Abimelech

In Genesis 20, we find the story of Abraham and Abimelech. Abimelech was a person of influence and means. Abraham feared

Abimelech and told Sarah to present herself as his sister and not his wife. Understanding her to be single, Abimelech took Sarah into his care with the intent of marrying her.

God revealed to Abimelech the truth about Sarah through a dream, so Abimelech confronted Abraham (more on Abimelech later). Abraham gave three excuses which we will look at in reverse order.

Abraham admitted that introducing Sarah as his sister was their normal procedure whenever they traveled or moved (Gen 20:13). Abraham had used this same tactic while in Egypt, telling Pharaoh that Sarah was his sister (see Gen. 12). After God sent plagues, Pharoah ran Abraham out of his land. We know he used this tactic at least twice, but the wording in Genesis 20 points to this having happened multiple times. In short, it was their agreed-upon practice.

They appear to have gotten accustomed to living a lie, giving us a clue about why we may not be grieved by sin. Over time, it just got easier to carry out this deception. In his first letter to Timothy, Paul pointed to a person's conscience being seared (1 Tim. 4:2). That word translated "seared" points to scar tissue that is no longer sensitive to touch, and that appears to be what happened to Abraham and Sarah. They were no longer sensitive to the guilt that comes with deception.

The test of conscience no longer applied. The test of conscience is that sense of guilt felt after committing a sin. It makes us stay up at night, replaying the actions over and over, with us wishing we could go back and do it a different way. However, if one does that same act a second time, it becomes easier, the searing has begun. Eventually there is no more sense of guilt because of the searing; we are no longer spiritually sensitive to our own conscience. That is where Abraham appeared to be in this episode in Genesis 20.

Abraham's second excuse was that he really did not tell a lie. (Gen. 20:12). It was only a half-truth. Half-truths can be more dangerous than an all-out lie because the person to whom we lie will create his own story based on the information given. The problem is we tend to create stories that are usually inaccurate, and that was exactly what Abraham was hoping would happen.

Abraham's first stated excuse is where we find the biggest issue. He characterized Abimelech and his people as pagan Gentiles unaware of the God who created them (Gen. 20:11). No effort was required by Abraham to label this group of people. He did not need to engage in meaningful dialogue or ask tough questions. Nor did he need to tell his story or listen to theirs. To be fair, Abimelech and his people seem to be comfortable with this, neither sharing the pains and scars that got them to that point.

Beyond the laziness was the arrogance expressed by Abraham. Behind this excuse is the attitude that Abimelech and his people were just pagan Gentiles, unlike Abraham who had several conversations with God. He viewed himself as superior.

Labeling another person is usually a license to mistreat that person and a means of avoiding any grief over sin. Abraham forgot that "they" are also created in God's image. Since in his mind they were less than human, he could then treat them as such. He forgot that God loves "them" just like He loved him.

Amazingly one thing we do not see is Abraham admitting that he was wrong. There appears to be no repentance. He confesses that he lied but does so in a way so that he was not required to change or feel guilt. He shows no grief about this sin. We may admit we did something but are not sorry or grieved for it. We would have expected more of Abraham. Genesis 15:6 points to him believing and being declared righteous as a result. In Genesis 20:7, God identified Abraham as a prophet, which is also the only time that word was used in Genesis; we will not see it again until Exodus 7:1 when Aaron is called the prophet of Moses or his mouthpiece. Even though Abraham was these things, he was not grieved by his sin.

We find a different portrait when we look at Abimelech. We find him taking Sarah to be his wife (Gen. 20:1–2). We are not told why he chose to take Sarah with the intent of marriage, but the intent was clear.

That night, God approached Abimelech in a dream, letting him know that Sarah was a married woman. Abimelech claimed ignorance, noting that he acted on the information given to him by Abraham. God acknowledged Abimelech's ignorance but also proceeded as if his ignorance was no excuse. The great flood and Sodom and Gomorrah both took place before God delivered the Ten Commandments (Exod. 20). Interestingly, Abimelech appeared to view taking a married woman to be a wife as wrong before the giving of the Ten Commandments as well.

So, how did he know what was wrong and right? In Jude 10 (NASB1995), we find the phrase "things which they know by instinct," and it is used in connection to sinful actions. The Bible tells us that we as humans know right from wrong even in this fallen state. Paul in his letter to the Romans in chapter 2 verse 14 declared that the Gentiles instinctively do the law without having the law. In this passage, we see Abimelech, understanding the wrongness of taking a woman who was married, knowing this to be adultery.

God revealed to Abimelech that He had kept him from spending the night with Sarah. God protected Abimelech from himself. God also provided a means of redemption for Abimelech. God is the One offended; He gets to set the terms. Abimelech was in no position to barter, nor did he attempt to do so. Abimelech needed a mediator, someone to vouch for him, on his behalf, and God designated Abraham as the one who would do that for Abimelech.

Unlike Abraham, Abimelech acted. He understood the gravity of his actions. He did not wait but followed God's directions first thing that morning. He even informed his advisors, making sure they understood the situation. They too would be impacted by Abimelech's actions.

Abimelech did what God directed him to do, and as a result God accepted him, and that was all that really mattered. He may have wondered if God would accept him especially when he fully understood the depth of his sins, grieving over them. He may have found comfort in God's accepting a habitual liar in Abraham, even calling him a prophet. Surely God would accept a repentant Gentile.

Both men were faced with their sin, yet Abimelech was the one who understood the gravity of the moment. Granted, God confronted Abimelech and not Abraham, but should that excuse Abraham from having the same kind of grief for his sin?

How Does Grief over Sin Develop?

Developing this mark starts with reading the Bible. Reading the Bible sounds so simple, but that is where we discover the heart of God. Daniel recorded a prayer in chapter 9 of the book that bears his name, in which he confessed the sins of God's people. That prayer was borne out of his reading of Scripture. Daniel tells us as much: "In the first year of Darius, the son of Ahasuerus, a Mede by birth, who was made king over the Chaldean kingdom—in the first year of his reign, I, Daniel, understood from the books according to the word of the Lord to the prophet Jeremiah that the number of years for the desolation of Jerusalem would be seventy. So I turned my attention to the Lord God to seek him by prayer and petitions, with fasting, sackcloth, and ashes" (Dan. 9:1–3).

Jeremiah presented this idea of a seventy-year duration twice, once prior to Babylon's invading Jerusalem and the second in a letter to the captives in Babylon (see Jer. 25:1–11 and 29:1–10). The people were told that they would serve the king of Babylon for seventy years before God would allow them to return to Jerusalem.

Daniel responded to the words God directed Jeremiah to pen by praying. He did the math. He was aware of the state of God's people living in exile, including himself, knowing they were not ready to return to the promised land. He confessed the sin of God's people, including himself in that number when most would see him as above reproach. All this started with his reading Jeremiah's prophecies.

Believe It

Beyond reading Jeremiah's prophecies, Daniel believed what he was reading. The majority of Jeremiah's book portrays God as rightly hurt by the actions of His people. But Jeremiah also included a message of hope as seen in the potter reforming the clay in Jeremiah 18 and the declaration in 51:5 that God had not forsaken His people even though their land was filled with guilt.

The Bible does not pull any punches when it comes to sin. All humans are sinful with one exception, Jesus. The world is filled with sin, and we contribute to that sin, adding to the pile of filth that already exists. This reality points to the need for the cross.

Nor does the Bible pull any punches when it comes to God's grace. God can and will redeem the worst of us from the pagan king to the self-righteous Pharisee. God offers life to those willing to follow His Son. This reality points to the victory of the resurrection.

Daniel believed what he read and acted, which leads us to the next step in learning to grieve over sin—ownership.

Own It

Owning it means we move from believing what we find in the Bible to asking how a truth changes the way we think, feel, act, and relate.

We saw in Abraham someone who admitted his actions but failed to own them. In Daniel we find a person who owned not only his sin but also the sin of his ancestors and relatives. While he may have grieved over the state of Jerusalem or the temple, his grief included personal ownership. We see this in the pronouns used by Daniel in his prayer in chapter 9. In verse 5, he stated that we have sinned. In verse 6, Daniel declares that we have not listened. In verses 7 and 8, he notes that shame belongs to us. In verse 15, he circles back and confesses we have sinned; we have acted wickedly.

No record exists of Daniel's being accused of any sin or egregious act. He did not kill an Egyptian in defense of a Hebrew, commit adultery while his army was out fighting, or lie about his wife being his sister. As best we can tell, Daniel is one of the few people in Scripture without a flaw, yet here he is saying *we* sinned. This is what it looks like to own sin.

Owning sin is painful. We don't want to see ourselves as the one who caused this mess. But ownership is the path to confession, repentance, and forgiveness. If we avoid the ownership, we will avoid the pain, but we will also avoid the joy of God's mercy. In repentance, we discover the joy and depth of God's grace. We also discover what Paul prayed for the Ephesians: that they may be able to comprehend the length and width, height and depth of God's love (Eph. 3:18).

We not only own our sin before God but also with ourselves and others. Daniel admitted that he was just as guilty as the kings who ignored the warnings of the prophets. Think about how hard that may have been for Daniel who was led away to Babylon as a teenager. Because of the decisions made by the leaders of Judah, he would have a vastly different future than what he had anticipated. Yet he owned their decision and disobedience, realizing he was just as capable of the same disobedience and, therefore, culpable.

By recording his prayer, Daniel was also owning his sin for others to see. In effect, he was confessing in such a way that all could see it, even us. Confessing to others not only sets an example and creates accountability, but it also frees us to own our sin in a deeper way. In writing this book, I was aware of a couple of issues that kept me from moving beyond this section. The block was removed once ownership of a specific sin was declared to a group of people. The sin related to a pain caused by someone else and how I responded to that pain. Admitting our sin can be painful. But freedom comes when we admit it because our ownership requires a trust in Jesus to cover our sin. Admitting that sin to trusted and respected people served as a means to declare that Jesus has covered the sin, and I have no shame in telling others because He is sufficient. Confession is one way we become part of the answer to Paul's prayer in Ephesians 3 that we would know *with the saints* the magnitude of God's love.

See Others with God's Heart

A side effect of owning sin is gaining love for others. This love comes out of our own repentance. The mercy we find in repentance becomes the great motivator. We discover God's heart that is warm to us, that longs for us to be with Him. We are grieved that we allowed sin to rob us of experiencing God's faithful love and are grieved that others allow sin to rob them of that same discovery. Our love for someone, even someone who hurt us deeply, is proportional to our willingness to be grieved over their sin in the same way we are grieved over our sin. Our being grieved over the sin of others opens the door to living out the heart of God who is merciful and expects us to be so as well, even to our enemies. Jesus also told His hearers not to judge or condemn but to forgive and give, following in the steps of the Teacher (see Luke 6:27–40).

Let me try to sum up the steps here. Read the Bible. Believe it. Own it (confess, which includes admit and repent and leads to a deeper ability to love). For me, it had to be done in this order. In the process, I discovered that grieving over sin and love are inseparable.

Your Turn

List sins of others that have caused you great hurt. Acknowledge to God the hurt and confess any response that does not honor God, asking Him to help you love them the same way you expect God to love you.

Take an honest look at sin and what it does to us by reading and reflecting on Psalm 38. What do you need to own before God, admitting and repenting of that sin?

Taking a Deeper Look

Using a Bible reference tool like a concordance or cross-reference, examine Bible passages that reference God's heart being broken, with Genesis 6 as a starting place. Be sure to read the verses before and after to get a clearer view of what is happening in the passage. How did reading these passages impact your view of sin?

Chapter 4

DEFERRED CONFIDENCE

People marked by prayer carry themselves with a deferred confidence.

Prior to 2008, professional football teams that won the coin toss prior to the beginning of a game had two choices: They could elect to receive or kick the ball to start the game or decide which end zone they would initially defend. Most decided to receive the ball to start the game. The rule was changed in 2008, giving a third option: to defer their selection to the second half. It took a few seasons, but in today's game the choice is nearly always to defer.

Choosing to defer should mean the deferring team closes out the first half with the ball and starts the second half with the ball, at least in theory. If that team can score on both of those possessions, that is a potential fourteen-point swing that can change the course of the game. It also forces the other team to receive the ball to start the game, placing the team that won the toss on defense first. If they have a strong defense planned for the opposition, they can set the tone for the game early. This strategy also means the deferring team can make adjustments at halftime based on what the other team did in the first half and begin the second half knowing the approach taken by the opposition's defense.

Deferring potentially places a football team in a better strategic position. To do so, they must surrender their choice at the start of the game. People marked by prayer also understand the strategic position of deferring and surrender.

To defer when talking about prayer is not delaying or putting off an action, as some might understand defer. Instead, we are talking about rightly delegating or submitting to another person's wishes, thoughts, or authority.

We usually think of delegating as an act taken by someone in a position of authority. A boss may delegate tasks, for example, to those he or she supervises. However, delegating can also be done in the opposite direction, from the bottom up, and that is what happens in the life of the person marked by prayer. When they face a decision or situation, they defer or delegate the decision or situation up to God. This delegation is an act of reverence and in recognition of His authority. We may define this action in terms of trusting God to be God. They turn to Him before acting, deciding, or speaking.

If we view deferring in terms of submitting, the person marked by prayer is surrendering to God. They have a will and desire, but they place their will and desire on hold in deference to God's will and desire. They have come to grips with three yes/no questions:

1. Do you believe God to be the Creator of the universe?

2. Do you believe God created with purpose and is active in His creation today?
3. Have you asked Him what He wants done in His creation today?

Behind each of these questions is the recognition of God's authority and a willingness to surrender to that authority.

In ancient European society, homage ceremonies became a ritual that served as the backbone to a feudal system. The vassal surrendered to the lord or king by kneeling and extending his joined hands forward and professing, "I am your man." The lord or king would then clasp the extended hands between his own hands, accepting the surrender.

Claude King points out that as Christians realized they had a heavenly King who deserved their loyalty more so than an earthly lord or king, they developed a new posture for prayer. They would get on one knee, place their palms together, and imagine they were placing their hands into the hands of King Jesus.[6] In effect, the bended knee with bowed head and praying hands was a declaration of surrender to God. Just as this homage ceremony marked a surrender, persons marked by prayer understand they too are surrendering through prayer.

Surrender ushers in a different source of authority. Vassals had the power of the monarch behind them when acting on their behalf. They now had a different authority that could be seen in how they demanded compliance from others. As believers, we carry God's authority into the situation as long as our actions reflect His intentions. This new authority fosters confidence.

Defining this trait included several term combinations. Confident humility, trusting humility, and humble confidence were a few of the leading candidates, in order. Each had its own downfall. For example, confident humility is one of those word combinations that catches our attention. It may rank up there with jumbo shrimp, only choice, small crowd, and definite maybe. Many leadership gurus use this term to describe being comfortable with one's strengths to the point that we can admit our shortcomings. If we follow this definition, our confidence is in ourselves, and that confidence produces the ability to admit where we fall short. Our strengths cover our weaknesses. The confidence is in the wrong place if the term is used in reference to prayer.

The person marked by prayer is confident in God and Him alone. The prayer is not a call for God to bless the efforts and desires of the person praying. Instead, the person praying is asking God to reveal His desires, His heart, so they can align themselves with what God shows them. They can then face the decision or situation with confidence, knowing that what they are doing reflects the heart of God.

This surrender also includes giving credit. The person marked by prayer is fully aware that God deserves the credit and not the one praying. God directed their thoughts and showed them His heart. God was the One answering and working.

This deferred confidence is also seen in how the person marked by prayer approaches a project. Most of us have been assigned a task and began to develop a plan to accomplish the task. We may consult others along the way, which we may have included in our plans as well. We may eventually pray, asking God to help us accomplish the task and for His blessing on our efforts. The person marked by prayer takes a different approach. They begin with prayer, asking God to direct their steps before making a plan. They look for situations in Scripture that might be connected to the task at hand or look for how God may be honored through the task. Each part of a developed plan is filtered through God's character, knowing that some actions could be taken that would be counter to His character.

The approach just described impacts how a person understands unanswered prayer. Many view an unanswered prayer in terms of God's failing to deliver or not completing the to-do list we presented to Him that day. This person treats God as the servant and not the One worthy of being served.

The person marked by prayer instead focuses on discovering God's heart and taking steps to align with what God shows them. As such, an answer to prayer is found in God's revealing His heart and not our checklist of wants being delivered. The person marked by prayer may have a checklist of prayer needs but does so in anticipation of God's revealing His desires for that person or situation. That is what deferred confidence is all about: confidence in God and trust in Him and His plans for His creation.

Deferred confidence marks the person of prayer because they understand themselves in relation to God. They understand that they are not God and therefore have limits. They also understand that sin impacts our ability to be objective. However, God invites us to oversee His creation, having invested heavily in redeeming us for that purpose. We are inadequate and flawed but accepted and invited by Him. As a result, we defer to Him, trusting that He will provide what is needed for us to fulfill our God-given assignments.

Joseph and Pharaoh

In Genesis 41, we find Pharaoh dreaming about seven well-fed cows grazing that were followed by seven different cows that were ugly and malnourished. The seven ugly cows consumed the fat cows. He had a second dream that same night about seven healthy heads of grain and seven heads of grain that were scorched. Like the ugly cows, the seven scorched heads consumed the healthy heads of grain. Once morning came, Pharaoh began looking for someone to tell him what these two dreams meant. His chief cupbearer told him about his experience with Joseph while imprisoned.

Pharaoh summoned Joseph to determine if he would be able to interpret his dreams. When asked, Joseph replied that he was not able but that God would give understanding (see Gen. 41:16). Here we have deferred confidence.

Most of us would have been tempted to tell Pharaoh we would be happy to get out of jail and help him understand his dreams. All Pharaoh needed to know was that Joseph could tell him the meaning of the dream; Pharaoh was not interested in how Joseph came to understand the dreams' meaning.

Pharaoh then proceeded to tell the dreams to Joseph. Upon hearing the dreams, God revealed to Joseph the meaning of the dreams. Joseph explained that the seven good cows and heads of grain represented seven prosperous years while the seven ugly cows and worthless heads of grain pointed to seven years of famine. The seven years of prosperity would be forgotten in the middle of the famine that followed those years.

In the middle of explaining the meaning, Joseph reminded Pharaoh that God was the one who had shown Pharaoh what was about to happen (v. 28). He ended the explanation by once again pointing to God as being the One who determined the crop production or lack thereof for the next fourteen years (see v. 32). Another example of deferred confidence.

At this point in the encounter, Joseph had done what Pharaoh asked, interpreting the meaning of the dreams. He could have stopped there, and no one would have faulted him. God had revealed the significance, and Joseph had delivered what God revealed. However, there was more. Action was needed based on God's revealed future.

We must assume that God also revealed to Joseph what needed to be done in response. Joseph shared a plan in which 20 percent of all the harvest in the seven good years would be stored for the seven years of famine that would follow. Commissioners would be needed to oversee this collection of grain and storehouses would need to be created.

Notice that Joseph did not present himself as the person qualified to take on this task. Instead, he left that up to Pharaoh. Once again, we find an example of deferred confidence. Joseph was confident Pharaoh would act on the information and do so wisely. Pharaoh was surrounded by his officials who also affirmed the plan presented by Joseph. Surely, one of these officials had the administrative ability to oversee this work and the commissioners who would be needed. We don't know if Joseph stayed in the middle of the group while Pharaoh and his officials affirmed the merit of the establishing of the commissioners or if Joseph faded to the background for the time being. What we do know is Joseph did not explicitly volunteer himself to be that person. We also know that Pharaoh realized someone with a connection to God was needed to do the task and that the only one present in the room who fit the bill was Joseph (v. 38).

This deferred confidence had developed over time in Joseph. This was not the same Joseph who had showed off his prize robe whenever he had the opportunity as a teenager. That version of Joseph was many miles and experiences ago. That jacket no longer existed in its former glory and was a distant memory. He had endured the mistreatment of his brothers, life as a slave in a foreign land, unwanted sexual advances, false accusations, and being forgotten in a prison. Joseph was now thirty years old (41:46). Two years had passed since he interpreted the dreams of the baker and cupbearer. He was seventeen when he was sold to slave traders by his brothers (see Gen. 37:2). The next thirteen years gave him plenty of time to think and consider his life. He remained faithful to God and those in authority over him as is evident in his refusal of the sexual advances made by Potiphar's wife. His confidence in God no doubt grew as did His understanding of God's heart. That understanding will be seen later in his life as he provides for the brothers who had sold him to the slave traders in the first place.

Serve Others

Throughout Joseph's life, we see the common theme of service. Serving others builds confidence in God and in our own abilities. Paul declared to Timothy that deacons who served well would acquire good standing and greater boldness (1 Tim. 3:13). Phillips translated this phrase in Paul's letter as "gaining confidence and freedom in the Christian faith." We might think of this as the Gideon effect. God gave Gideon different assignments with each completed action, building confidence and faith in God. My dad's life demonstrated this reality. He served people by selling them auto parts and by sharing his expertise. He was also a deacon who served well. As he served, he became more comfortable speaking to others about Jesus. Serving gained him a willing ear, and thus he was more confident and bolder. Serving also taught him he could trust God more deeply, which led to greater boldness in sharing Jesus with others.[7]

The bottom line is serving others requires us to defer to others. We defer our schedule and interests so we can serve them. As we develop the habit of deferring to others through service in our daily lives, our approach to God will be impacted. As we defer to people, we more easily defer to God.

Credit Others

Joseph was quick to point out that God was the One who told him the meaning of the dreams. He gave credit where credit was due. We want to be aware of the dangers of failing to defer. We see the danger in the life of Herod who refused to defer credit to God after giving a speech to which the crowd reacted by declaring Herod to be a god (see Acts 12). Failing to defer to God cost Herod his life.

Looking for ways to give others their due credit fosters this trait with carryover into all areas of our life. When we are recognized for an accomplishment, we can point to others who assisted or played a role.

Some can argue that this attitude comes as a result of deferring to God, but it may be a both/and. We develop this habit in all our relationships, looking for what others contributed. We can begin by looking for ways to rightly credit others, knowing that doing so will impact our spiritual life as well.

Examine Motives

In Mark 1:12, we find Jesus being driven into the wilderness for a time of testing. When comparing translations, we find the terms "driven out," "impelled," "compelled," "forced Him out," "made Him go," and "put Him out." The Greek word Mark used to describe this sending is also found in reference to driving out a demon (Mark 6:13 is one example). The Holy Spirit was the one pushing Jesus into the wilderness.

Jesus had a great deal to say about motives in His Sermon on the Mount. Phrases like "when you pray," "when you fast," and "storing treasures on earth" all connect to a person's why. It is all about motive and what we trust. Our why may be more important than our what or how.

As we look at our motives, a few diagnostic questions can help. Here are three to get us started:

- Who gets the credit?
- Whom did I tell about what I did and why?
- How did I tell them what I did?

(Tip: Look for nouns and verbs used and the order they were used. For example, are you more likely to say, "I notified them of the issue," or, "They were notified about the issue"? The nouns, verbs, and order matter.)

Seek God's Direction

We touched on this earlier, but we need to pray first, knowing the contents of that prayer matter. Instead of asking God to bless our plans, we need to ask Him to show us His plans and our role in His plan being carried out. Recording our prayers in some type of journal gives us a tool to clearly see if our prayers are sincere efforts of seeking God's direction. We can review what we recorded and evaluate our prayers. We can ask God to help us see blind spots where we prayed for Him to bless and adopt our direction versus times when we voiced a true seeking of His will and direction.

Pray Without Ceasing

One more action needs our attention before moving on. Paul called on the Thessalonians to pray without ceasing. Lots could be said here, but let's focus on a practical way of doing this using colors. When we read the Bible each day and identify how God reveals Himself to us in that passage, we can assign a color to that characteristic of God. Let's say we read Psalm 69, which is a call for God to rescue His faithful. In verse 9, the psalmist called for God to rescue him from the miry mud. We may choose a dark brown to remind us of our need to be rescued from the muck of this world. As we go through the day, anytime we see the color dark brown, we can thank God for the salvation He provides through faith in Jesus and acknowledge our dependence on Him for that rescue. That color reminds us to focus our prayer on what God has most recently revealed to us about Himself. This builds a deferred confidence as we pray through the day in light of His Word.

Your Turn

Identify some type of service action you can take in which no one will be able to pay you back or know it was you who performed the act of service. After completing the act, covenant with yourself to tell no one about the act of service. Reflect on the emotions felt and times you were tempted to tell another person about what you did. What did you learn about yourself through this experience?

Review the Bible passage most recently examined in a Bible study group you attended. What was the main point about God's character? What color would you associate with that character trait? As you go through the day, look for that color as a reminder to pray in light of that character trait of God.

Digging Deeper

Spend some time reflecting on Psalm 131. Be sure to review the life of David using a Bible dictionary to remind yourself of some of his accomplishments. How is deferred confidence seen in this psalm?

Chapter 5

PRESENCE MINDED

People marked by prayer are consumed with being in the presence of God.

Advanced Greek II was one of the more challenging classes taken in college. This class was really a series of classes that covered four semesters over two years. It was open only to juniors and seniors since you had to successfully complete two years of Greek prior to enrolling. Advanced Greek II was considered an elective but recommended for those seeking a degree in biblical studies.

Over the two years of that series of classes, students would work toward translating the book of Ephesians, three chapters a year. Most would only get to do one year because of the prerequisites, but a few were able to do both years. It was offered only once per semester, so students had to plan all their other courses around it. Homework was required prior to every class time, no exception. The students would parse and diagram the passage assigned for that class and then be prepared to present their work to the rest of the class. They may not be the one called on that day, but they had to be ready nonetheless. There was no final test given so every class time counted toward the final grade.

For the students who took the course all four semesters, they would have a full set of translation notes on the book of Ephesians. The greater value was getting to study Ephesians with the professor who taught it. He would engage you in conversation about the process you followed to create your translation, offer insights into how he addressed the same passage, and help you process how each approach impacted the larger understanding of Paul's letter. The class was small, so you got to know that professor in a deeper way, and he got to know you. Gaining insight from this professor was the greater value in taking the class or series of classes. We got to be in his presence and glean from his wisdom while wrestling with how to translate Ephesians. He was also the dean of the department, which didn't hurt.

Many have a teacher or professor they looked up to when in school. Some may have chosen to take classes from that teacher or professor knowing the challenges that would come with doing so. However, we may have overlooked the challenge since we revered that teacher or knew we would gain a great deal from them. We also invested more into those classes, making sure we were prepared if called on in the class and that assignments were on time and typo-free. We were there to learn from that person, knowing that they had something to offer that other instructors did not. We were less likely to question or debate them on a point, trusting they had done the research. Their expertise compelled us to take the class in the first place. We might ask for clarification, doing so with respect, being careful not to cast doubt on what the teacher or professor was proposing. Somehow, we also made it to that class on time, wanting to get as much time with that teacher as possible. Arriving early also put us in a position to visit with that teacher prior to the official start of class. That teacher may not always arrive early, but when they did, we were ready. The reason for enrolling in that class was all about being in the presence of that teacher or professor. If they knew our name, in a good way, that only added to the experience.

People marked by prayer have this same view of God. They desire to be in His presence, knowing that He will give them truth for that day or for whatever they are facing. They are not there to question Him although they may raise questions. Nor are they there to tell Him what to do, but instead they want to ask for His counsel on the things they and others are facing.

This desire to be in God's presence develops out of deferred confidence since they are keenly aware that God is at work around and through them. And they want to be aware of that presence again—to see God at work in a fresh way.

Being in God's presence can be scary just like being in the class of that revered teacher. We take the risk of that revered teacher asking us a question and of our work not meeting standards. That is one reason we double-check our papers before submitting them. For the person marked by prayer, they too understand the scary side of being in God's presence.

They are aware that they are not worthy of being in God's presence. God is holy and we are not. The Bible tells us that God is light, and in Him is no darkness. Light can be scary for those of us who have things we have put in the dark corner of a closed closet. We would rather those things not be exposed by the light. What happens if those things become the focus of our conversation with the Father? Are we willing to take that risk?

But people marked by prayer are drawn to the light of God's presence. More than drawn, they hunger for that presence. They return to locations where they encountered God in the past. These places are holy to them, but they are not replacements for God. It is not about the location but who was present at that location. They know exactly where they were in that room or area. They may have even left a mark so they could find the location again in the future.

For people marked by prayer, a strange contentment is found in God's presence. We see this contentment expressed in Psalm 17:14–15 as David ended his request: "With your hand, Lord, save me from men, from men of the world whose portion is in this life: You fill their bellies with what you have in store; their sons are satisfied, and they leave their surplus to their children. But I will see your face in righteousness; when I awake, I will be satisfied with your presence."

David recognized that some would only find contentment when they had possessions that could be passed to the next generation. But he realized that those were things that only satisfy in this life, which is why those things are passed on to children; we cannot take those things with us. David instead sought contentment in something, really Someone, who could bring contentment in this life and the life to come.

We like to think about the inheritance we have as children of God. We focus on the streets of gold and mansions. We think of a life of ease surrounded by all that is perfect. David had a different view of that inheritance. He declared in Psalm 16:5 that God is his inheritance. God is the perfect and everlasting inheritance promised to us. As such, it is about being in His presence, and those marked by prayer understand this better than most.

Though their prayer may include the presenting of a list of needs to the Father, prayer is so much more than that. Prayer is being in the presence of God with an open heart ready to follow His directives. We may ask for clarity but are careful to do so with respect. People marked by prayer understand that being in God's presence on the earth is a foretaste of what it means for God to be our eternal inheritance. This is the secret, the critical element, required for being marked by prayer—an overwhelming desire to be in the presence of God.

A View from Two Marys

We see this desire to be in God's presence in the lives of two women both named Mary. The first of these Marys lived in Bethany, just a short walk southeast of Jerusalem. Jesus escaped to Bethany several times in His life finding refuge there, usually in the house of Mary's family. In one of His visits recorded in Luke 10, we find Mary and her sister contrasted. Martha was burdened by the duties of hosting guests, while Mary sat in on the conversation at the feet of Jesus. Seeing her sister leaving her to do all the work was too much for Martha to bear. She approached Jesus about

Mary's dereliction of duty as cohost. Jesus reminded Martha that few things were really needed for the hosting to take place. He also affirmed Mary for having chosen to sit at His feet.

Mary enjoyed being in the presence of Jesus. Her actions showed it to the frustration of Martha. Martha is seen as uptight and busy. Mary was relaxed, immersed in the deep conversation with Jesus. Mary had tasks to be done, but those paled in comparison to being in the presence of Jesus.

That same contentment in the presence of God was expressed at the death of their brother, Lazarus. Both Martha and Mary expressed confidence that if Jesus had been present a few days earlier, then Lazarus would not have died (see John 11:21, 32). Both women understood the power of Jesus's presence. They both knew that His presence changes a situation.

John conveyed another story about Mary that points to her desire to be in God's presence. In John 12, we are told that Mary anointed the feet of Jesus with some precious oil. Mary seemed to have a deeper understanding of Jesus's destiny and purpose than even the disciples and especially Judas at this time. Included in that awareness was an understanding on some level that the physical presence of Jesus would soon end for her and the others in that room. Jesus even stated as much, responding when confronted: "Leave her alone; she has kept it for the day of my burial. For you always have the poor with you, but you do not always have me" (John 12:7–8). Instead of waiting for the burial, Mary acted when Jesus was present.

A second Mary who valued the presence of Jesus was Mary of Magdala. She was from a trade center on the western shore of the Sea of Galilee. Mark and Luke reveal that Jesus delivered this Mary from seven demons (see Mark 16:9; Luke 8:2). His presence set her free from the demons that had controlled her, and she became one of Jesus's biggest supporters. Her name appears first when women followers of Jesus are listed, leading some to believe she was the chief financial supporter of Jesus. She accompanied Jesus, as did some other women, on His journey from Galilee to Jerusalem. She was there the final week of Jesus's earthly life.

Most of Jesus's entourage abandoned Him at the crucifixion with a few notable exceptions: the "beloved disciple," better known as John, and several women including Mary of Magdala. Displaying courage, she remained at the foot of the cross as Joseph of Arimathea and Nicodemus removed the body, wrapped it in cloth, and placed it in a borrowed tomb. She observed it all and knew precisely where the body had been placed.

Early Sunday morning, Mary of Magdala led a team of women to the tomb to complete the preparation of Jesus's body for permanent burial. Per John's account, Mary was the first to arrive at the empty tomb (see John 20:1–18). Astonished and confused, she sought out Peter to tell him of her discovery. Peter and John went to see for themselves and found the linen cloth that had once wrapped the body neatly folded inside. Peter left confused while John left believing.

Upon her return to the tomb, Mary was the first to encounter the angels who declared Jesus to be resurrected. Then she encountered who she thought to be the gardener. We are not told why she interpreted the presence of the other person as the gardener, only that she asked him if he knew the whereabouts of the body or Jesus. She offered to take the body, presumably to give the body an appropriate burial.

The mood of that day changed when the One she understood to be the gardener called her by name. She now knew the identity of the other person present; it was Jesus. She addressed Him in Aramaic, calling Him "Rabboni" (a strong word meaning Master or Lord). Mary fell at His feet and clung to them with all she had.

Mary understood the value of being in His presence. She could join the sons of Korah when they declared: "I long and yearn for the courts of the LORD; my heart and flesh cry out for the living God. . . . Better a day in your courts than a thousand anywhere else. I would rather stand at the threshold of the house of my God than live in the tents of wicked people" (Ps. 84:2, 10).

Jesus had to direct Mary to stop holding on to Him so she could go tell the disciples that He would be returning to the Father to take His rightful place. Nothing seemed more important to Mary than being in the presence of Jesus at that point. He had to command Mary to let go so she could go tell others about His resurrection. In obedience, she let go and reported her encounter to the disciples.

Mary had been at the right place to encounter Jesus. She knew where His body had been laid and was confident that she had returned to the correct tomb. Where else would one expect to find Him? She placed herself in a position to be in the presence of God.

Both Marys give us a glimpse of what it looks like to be consumed with being in the presence of God. Both had very different experiences and encounters. The same is true for others who encountered God, which brings us to how we foster that desire for being in the presence of God.

No Formula

There is no formula to follow that assures us that God will show up for us. We don't find a step 1, step 2 approach that leads to the throne. God will show up when God wants to show up; He is God.

God appeared to Moses in a burning bush in a desert. He would appear to Moses again on a mountain with Moses needing to wear a veil afterwards as a result. Isaiah saw the throne of God in a vision and responded with repentance and a commitment to go. Samuel was awakened by a voice that called for him in the night. Elijah was running away from perceived danger, and God appeared to him with a whisper that followed a mighty wind, earthquake, and fire. Paul was blinded by a bright light on the road to Damascus.

This appearance to Paul was so life-changing for Paul that it is recorded in three places in Acts (chapters 9; 22; and 26). In his letter to the Philippians, Paul declared that his goal was to know God and His power (Phil. 3:10). He was not looking for fame or recognition but for the face of the One who appeared to him on the way to Damascus. That encounter changed everything for Paul.

While each of these encounters listed are different, one thing is constant—God showing up and making His presence known.

Obstacles

Some specific things get in the way of God being present. The first of these is sin. We are told by Jesus that we should get things right with others before delivering an offering to the Lord (Matt. 5:22–23). Isaiah declared that the sin of the people nullified their religious practices including fasting (see Isa. 58:3ff) and that their sin was the reason God did not listen to them (Isa. 59:2). Sin is not always the reason God is silent, but sin can be one reason we do not find ourselves in God's presence, nor do we want to be in His presence at that point.

A second reason can be neglect. Redemption is about a relationship with the Father. Ignoring a relationship never strengthens that relationship. Absence does not make the heart fonder. When the exiled Israelites returned to Jerusalem, they were excited about restoring the city. Cyrus allowed the exiles to return in 538 BC, and they began construction on the temple two years later. That initial work lasted for two years and then ceased. They worked hard on the walls and their homes while the temple sat silent. Haggai was sent to challenge the people to give attention to rebuilding their spiritual lives. For the next fourteen years the temple sat unfinished and neglected. They were busy doing everything else required to rebuild but neglecting the centerpiece.

A third thing that can get in the way of God's showing up is assumption. We may assume that God will always be there when we need Him. The people of Judah believed they were safe as long as the temple was present and maintained. They assumed God would appear and rescue them from whatever threat they faced as a result. While a form of neglect, assumption goes deeper since we suddenly stop neglecting Him and expect Him to respond whenever we deem Him needed.

Fostering the Desire

So, if there is no formula to follow and we know there are some things that can get in the way, what are we to do to foster this desire to be in God's presence? Notice that we did not say how we could control or dictate God's presence but rather how we could foster a desire to be in His presence. We don't control God and His timing. We do control how we foster our desire for Him.

First, we can address any sin including our ignoring and assumption of God. We dealt with confession earlier when addressing grief over sin, which is a first step here. After our confession and repentance, we then take the next step of abiding in Him, spending time with the Father.

In addition to spending time with Him, we follow His directions. The call to be a disciple of Jesus is built on following Him. We are not called to lead Him, walk beside Him, or stay on a path from a safe distance. Instead, we are called to follow Him closely, stepping in the footprints He just vacated. When we follow closely, we may not be able to see what lies immediately ahead so we must trust the person we are following to navigate that for us.

As we follow Him, we are to stay alert not only to where He steps next but also to what is going on around us. Many times we fail to see God working in and around us by simply not being alert.

Moses was doing his everyday thing, watching sheep, when he came across the burning bush. We don't know when God will make His presence known or how, so we must remain alert for when He does.

To be fair, most of us will never be walking in the wilderness and encounter a burning bush. However, we may see Him working in the relationships and conversations we have throughout the day. We may sense His work in us as we dialogue with a friend facing a challenging time and the passage we read that morning providing the perfect encouragement to that friend. We may see it in asking God to guide our steps as we do some work and then realize He is bringing together the pieces. The issue is remaining aware as we follow Jesus.

One more thing to remember is to seek God's counsel as we follow. While on a group bike ride, we may follow another rider who is more experienced. However, asking them for tips as to the value of staying in the saddle while climbing may give us greater insight than just watching. The assumption here is that we are following Jesus close enough to tap Him on the shoulder to ask Him for His thoughts.

Your Turn

Ask God to show you if there are any obstacles in your life that keep you from entering God's presence. If there are any, take the actions needed to remove them.

Set aside some time to simply read a section of the Psalms. Express to God the truths found about Him and how you see those characteristics playing out in your own experience. Thank Him for showing His character to you.

Dig Deeper

Set aside some time to read Genesis 3 and 4; Genesis 34; Isaiah 6; 1 Samuel 3; 1 Kings 19; and Acts 9. Record insights you gained about God and His presence. How does reading these stories encourage you to seek God's presence?

Chapter 6

FOUNDATION

The marks grow out of a willingness to follow Jesus no matter what.

We have examined five characteristics of believers marked by prayer. The five marks work together, and one wonders if there is any prerequisite to securing these marks. Is there another reality working in the background? Does the securing of these marks begin with a sense of helplessness, or is there something else that must be noted?

In all my reading and reflection, one reality surfaced that impacts being marked by prayer. More realities may impact the journey along the way, but one specific reality determines if a person will start and end the journey of being marked by prayer. This reality is foundational for all five marks, and it is the level of our willingness to follow Jesus no matter what.

Fort Campbell is located on the Kentucky and Tennessee state line. The 101st Airborne Division, among others, calls this U.S. Army base home. The base is named after William Bowen Campbell, who was a noted politician in Tennessee history. When the Mexican-American war began in 1846, Tennessee's governor, Aaron Brown, issued a call for volunteers. Campbell answered that call and was selected to be colonel of the First Tennessee Volunteers. This group saw action in several battles including the Battle of Monterrey. Needing to make an advance on Fort Taneria, Campbell led his troops into the battle, giving the command, "Boys, follow me!" They endured heavy losses, earning the nickname of the "Bloody First," but they were also successful in accomplishing their mission that day, being the first over the walls and into the fort. "Boys, follow me!" became Campbell's campaign slogan when he successfully ran for governor of Tennessee in 1851.

The declaration of "Follow me" by a military leader sets a clear direction. The soldiers knew exactly what was expected. They were aware that military success is built on a chain of command; you receive orders and you execute. You may be following or asked to lead in response to an order. The assumption is that one person leads and the others follow.

Following a specific person removes at least one stress on the battlefield. Soldiers talk about the chaos of battle and need for clarity. Knowing to follow a specific person helps as the battle presses. You follow that leader, and that is how you will be evaluated. Failure to follow puts the mission in danger as well as you and the others depending on you.

Following also changes the question of responsibility. Your responsibility is to follow. You are not asked to decide if the attack should be to the right, left, or in the middle. That decision is someone else's to make. Your task is to follow and to make sure everyone else can follow as well. You don't even need to know the objective; you just need to know whom to follow, removing some of the complexity for you.

Behind that willingness to follow a person into battle is a trust that the person leading knows where to go and why. You trust that they are taking the right action. You know they may be leading you into danger and are willing to follow anyway because of that trust. You trust them to navigate the danger while you follow. You hope to follow them out of the danger, but you follow not knowing if that will be the case. The assignment is to follow.

The Bible uses a variety of terms to define a person in good standing with God. We are called soldiers, children, and sheep, to name a few. Each of these three listed carries the idea of following. Sheep or a flock is one of the more common images used in Scripture. We are led beside still waters in Psalm 23, listen for the voice of the Shepherd in John 10:14, and are sought when lost in Matthew 18. We are told that His sheep hear the Shepherd's voice and follow Him (John 10:27).

Being a follower of Jesus defines what we are to be and do. We are believers for sure, but we are more than a person who accepts (believes) the facts about Jesus and His teachings, death, and resurrection. We follow Him.

Mark introduced the idea of following Jesus early in his Gospel. In chapter 1, we find Jesus calling Simon and Andrew to follow Him with the promise of making them fishers of men (Mark 1:17). They left their livelihood and followed. Levi, also known as

Matthew, was given the same invitation in Mark 2:14, also leaving behind his tax booth and following.

In Mark 8, we find Jesus addressing a crowd along with His disciples. He challenged them to deny themselves, take up a cross, and follow Him (v. 34). Jesus had just explained that He would face persecution and death, yet be raised after three days. Peter took Jesus aside to correct Him only to have Jesus rebuke Peter for failing to set his focus on the things of God. Jesus directed Peter to "get behind me, Satan" (Matt. 16:23), another way of saying, "Follow me" (Matt. 16:24).

In Mark 10, we find a rich young ruler approaching Jesus with a question about inheriting eternal life. Jesus pointed to some of the commandments, which the young man claimed to have kept. Jesus directed the young man to sell his possessions, give the proceeds to the poor, and then to follow Him. The young man left grieving, unable to take that action. God used this passage in Mark 10 to draw me to Himself as a sixteen-year-old. I did not want my story to end the same way it did for the rich young ruler.

The initial decision to follow Him serves as the first step. But following is more than a one-time decision. Luke's account of the conversation recorded in Mark 8 includes the word *daily* with the phrase "taking up one's cross" (see Luke 9:23). While the word is specific to taking up one's cross, since each action is connected, we can assume there to also be a daily element in denying ourselves and following.

For the person marked by prayer, they daily express a commitment to follow Jesus. Their salvation is secure, but how that salvation is lived out on that specific day is the issue. Peter was invited to follow Jesus and would continue to hear that invitation even after the resurrection. John told about the disciples fishing and seeing the resurrected Jesus on the shore. Peter swam ashore to find Jesus preparing breakfast and ready to initiate a conversation. Jesus asked Peter about his love for Him and challenged Peter to feed His lambs, shepherd His sheep, and feed His sheep. After being told that he would honor God as a martyr, Peter was directed by Jesus once again to follow Him (see John 21:19). In response, Peter asked about the future of John, and Jesus met Peter's question with the same direction as before: Follow Me (John 21:22). Peter was being called upon to follow Jesus no matter what and to do so daily.

People marked by prayer view salvation as more than a moment in time past when they publicly declared their need for forgiveness and their desire to trust Jesus. The day they began following Jesus is important, but so is today. They identify with Peter, knowing Jesus repeats that call to follow Him daily.

The call to follow no matter what was not new or unique to Peter. Many others faced the same decision, including Habakkuk.

Habakkuk

Habakkuk gives us a glimpse into his prayer journal, providing a set of specific prayer notes. The exchange began by Habakkuk asking why God would allow sin to continue without intervening to stop it (1:1–3). Habakkuk appears to have recorded this prayer exchange in the days following King Josiah's death. Josiah had led Judah, the southern kingdom, to return to God. When the Egyptian army began to move to help the Assyrians, Josiah disguised himself to do battle with the Egyptians, and it cost him his life. His death created a leadership vacuum that opened the door for the people to abandon God and return to idolatry. Habakkuk was witnessing the undoing of the spiritual revival that had taken place under Josiah, and he could not understand why God was letting this happen. He asked why he was forced to look at injustice as God tolerated the wrongdoing going on (see Hab. 1:2).

Habakkuk's questions were legitimate. We can certainly understand the feelings expressed in this prayer. God does not shy away from our hard questions, and He did not shy away from giving Habakkuk a response. God revealed to the prophet that He was going to punish Judah for their sin, and He would use the Babylonians to do so. God even began His response by warning Habakkuk that he would not believe what he was about to be told (see Hab. 1:5).

Habakkuk responded, recording his thoughts in Habakkuk 1:12–2:1. The thought of the Babylonians being used by God to judge Judah was beyond Habakkuk's ability to swallow. He acknowledged that God was holy and that was the problem. Using a group more wicked to punish the less wicked, in Habakkuk's opinion, made little sense in his theological structures. He had already acknowledged that sin was out of control, but he expected God to do something other than use a pagan nation to bring discipline.

Habakkuk was rebuking God at that point. In effect, he was telling God He was wrong. He was informing God how He should act, reminding Him that He was holy and too pure to do what He had just said He would do.

Chapter 2 points to a defining moment. Habakkuk could have walked away from God, disappointed by God's perceived inconsistency and injustice. He would turn his back on God, discounting Him as being less than who he thought God should be. Or the prophet could sit and wait, trusting God to answer. The final words of this prayer (v. 1) indicate that Habakkuk chose the second option.

Make no mistake about who was in charge here. All the prophet could do was sit and wait for an answer. The ball was in God's court. Habakkuk was learning the other side of prayer that we tend to forget. Billboards on several highways proclaim, "Pray, God listens." While this is true, it only tells half of the story. The other half is: "Pray, God speaks," and Habakkuk was learning this the hard way.

God replied and began by telling Habakkuk to write down what He was going to say. Whenever we are told to write something down, we are usually the one who needs to read it more than the one who tells us to write. God's statement was clear. The Babylonians would be punished for their sin too, and it would happen on God's timetable.

Habakkuk received a more important message: that the righteous one will live by faith (Hab. 2:4). This statement is another way of inviting Habakkuk to follow Him. God does not need to explain Himself, and we are not in a position to demand such an explanation. Habakkuk needed to let God be God, trusting in Him even when following Him could be difficult or when we just do not understand.

Paul quotes Habakkuk 2:4 in Romans 1:17 and Galatians 3:11 to remind his readers that the Christian's life from beginning to end is based on faith. The writer of Hebrews references Habakkuk 2:4 as well, calling on the readers to remain steady in their trust in Jesus as they face persecution (see Heb. 10:38).

Habakkuk had a decision to make: Would he willingly follow God no matter what? He responded with a psalm that acknowledged God's sovereignty in dealing with sin as He saw fit and in His timing. The psalm ends with the prophet committing to remain faithful to following the Lord even when life was hard and when there were more questions than answers. God's power and goodness were to be sufficient, knowing that God was the source of strength.

Now Habakkuk was in a position to be marked by prayer. His questions were not wrong or misguided, but his allegiance needed to be reshaped. Once he could declare that he would follow God regardless, then he was back on the path to being marked by prayer.

When we begin our day with a renewed commitment to follow Jesus, the goal of our prayers is no longer telling God what He will and will not do that day but rather discerning what He wants us to do so we can follow. The items on our list may continue to be the same, but how we approach God with those items will be different.

Meet Susie. She was marked by prayer, bringing encouragement to others through prayer. Her life had many twists and hurts, but like Habakkuk, she had discovered the freedom found in a willingness to follow Jesus no matter what. She was one of the first to be enlisted to pray for me on a designated day each month. Some months, projects were purposefully scheduled on that day knowing she would be the one praying.

She had faced several surgeries and was facing yet another. She reached out by text asking for prayer, which led to a phone conversation. We visited about her surgery, caught up on a few things, reminded each other of our need to trust God no matter what, and then prayed. Her prayer was that she would be able to accept whatever God had for her on the other side of this surgery. She hoped for success but also knew the risks. She told God that she was ready for whatever was ahead even if that meant depending on someone else to help her get around the rest of her life. She also told God that she was just as ready to see Him as she was to walk with no pain and was leaving what awaited her in His hands. She was willing to follow Jesus no matter what.

This willingness to follow Jesus no matter what is the X factor for being marked by prayer. Shadrach, Meshach, and Abednego expressed this willingness when confronted about their failure to bow down to the king's image. When given an opportunity to make it up to the king by bowing the next time the instruments played, they responded: "Nebuchadnezzar, we don't need to give you an answer to this question. If the God we serve exists, then he can rescue us from the furnace of blazing fire, and he can rescue us from the power of you, the king. But even if he does not rescue us, we want you as king to know that we will not serve your gods or worship the gold statue you set up" (Dan. 3:16–18).

In short, they were expressing their willingness to follow God no matter what on that day. Habakkuk was called to do the same.

Connection Between Following and Prayer

Bicycle riding is an outlet for me. Riding gets me outside, moving, and away from my computer and email. Participating in organized rides keeps me motivated and disciplined in the everyday rides. One of these organized rides included a memorable encounter with a tandem bike team. Our group had joined up with the tandem riders a few miles into the ride. As we approached a turn, the rider in the front informed the other rider that they were approaching a turn and gave the direction and an angle. This continued as we rode. We came to a stop sign where the front rider then told the back rider they were about to stop and which foot to unclick first to put on the ground. After stopping, he then informed the back rider that all was clear, and they would continue riding in 3-2-1. Eventually, a person in our group asked about the giving of the commands. The back rider let us know that he was blind and needed the first rider to direct him. We discovered that this ride was the fifth such ride for the back rider and the twentieth for the front rider. They had trained together for three months in preparation for that day. The back rider knew he had to follow every directive if he was to succeed.

The Bible tells us that we are spiritually blind apart from faith in Jesus. While our initial faith in Him opens our eyes to spiritual truth (see 2 Cor. 4:1–6; John 12:40), we continue to have relapses and blind spots. Our understanding is also limited, with Habakkuk being an example.

When we approach life with a willingness to follow Jesus no matter what, we become like the blind rider of the tandem bike. We must listen and follow the directions given if we are to succeed. We must learn to trust Jesus, knowing He will give us the direction needed when we need it. That also means we approach prayer differently. We don't need to know about a turn fifteen miles down the road but instead about the one we are about to take. We can't see all the potholes and dangers, so we must trust Him to tell us when to turn and which foot to use when we come to a crossroad. Following becomes the focus of our prayer as opposed to our letting Him know what we see so He can fix it.

Following settles who is in charge and where we are headed. Following simplifies life for us since our responsibility is to simply take the next step. Following also implies presence. We can't follow someone with whom we do not have contact. Jesus offers to lead, but we must get in step, staying close enough—"abiding," as Jesus called it—to hear the direction. The closer we are, the greater the assurance that we can take the next step no matter what that step may be.

Building the Foundation

To be marked by prayer, we need to be a follower of Jesus. The intent is not to raise doubts for you but to challenge you to consider and reflect on your commitment to Jesus. Several references are made in this book about me making a commitment to follow Jesus as a teenager. I grew up going to church and knew all the answers to the questions. My journey included being baptized as a fifth grader based on my response to a select set of questions. For me, that was an intellectual exercise that was easy to pull off. The goal was to keep answering the questions.

God used a series of events to get my attention, which also pushed me to Mark's Gospel. The four "follow Me" passages were the critical pieces, causing me to examine my life through the lens of a follower. Becoming a follower of Jesus was the missing piece of my life. That commitment changed everything. No longer was I simply a believer of facts, but I was now a follower of Jesus.

That first step gave way to needing to daily declare an intent to follow Jesus. Some days are easier than others to make that declaration. Each morning now begins with gratitude to the Father for another day and a promise to willfully follow where He wants to lead on that day. My following is not contingent on how well I did the day before or what my plans may be for tomorrow but rather a specific reminder to myself that today, this day, will be a day for following Jesus.

My prayer time is now dominated by discovering where God wants to take me today in response to what He reveals to me that morning from His Word. My intent is to then filter any requests for that day through how He reveals Himself. My practice has not always been like this, but He has shaped my morning practices to help me be a more complete follower today than I was yesterday.

Your Turn

Reflect on the four passages from Mark that call for someone to follow Jesus (Mark 1:17; 2:14; 8:34; 10:21). Notice actions taken in response to each call to follow Him. Which person or group do you most identify with? How would you describe your life in terms of "follower of Jesus"?

On a scale of 0 to 10 with 0 being none and 10 being fully, how would you rate your willingness to follow Jesus today no matter what? What action might you take today to increase your willingness to follow Him?

CONCLUSION

Where do we go from here?

God has been kind to me, allowing me to be a part of some wonderful churches and serve in multiple ways. He has allowed me to see Him do some mighty things that opened doors for me to help other leaders. God allowed me to be in a church that grew by a thousand people in attendance over a five-year period. God used a lot of resources to make that happen in that church. Staffing, city culture, and a variety of other things came together for that church to be driven with a passion to reach people with the gospel. We saw college students, convicted felons, a satanist, and many others become faithful followers of Jesus. Several of us joined the staff at the beginning of those five years, giving the appearance that we were major contributors to that growth. Several of us were then asked to write articles and lead conferences explaining what we were doing. As those invitations began to come, the challenge was figuring out what we were actually doing that contributed to the growth. Obviously, God used us and our talents to impact what was going on. We were faithful to training people, to looking for ways to reach out in our community, to starting new Bible study groups, and to giving outreach a priority, but those were actions others were taking and not seeing the same results.

The answer to why the growth was taking place came on an early Saturday morning when I went to the church parking lot to meet a group of men for a golf outing. To my surprise, another group of men were already in the church facilities. It was a smaller group comparably, no more than ten men. They had keys to the building, which was unusual to say the least. They met in the building every Saturday morning to pray. They prayed for what would happen the next day, for God to remove obstacles for those who needed the Sunday school lesson and sermon, and for the people who would be leading the classes and worship. This smaller group met regardless of the weather or the season. Not all would be present every week, but some would. Their only purpose was to pray; there was no coffee or food present. They had been faithfully doing just that for several years. The church had been steady during those years, but what was happening at that point was what these men had been asking God to do from the first day they met to pray. They were finally seeing God answer the prayer they had begun voicing several years earlier.

People were aware of this group of praying men, with most being impressed by their consistency but not impressed enough to make the commitment to join them. To be fair, they invited others to join them but did so with humility and without fanfare. They did not brag about what they were doing; instead they faithfully carried out the task of asking God to impact their city . . . every Saturday morning . . . for years. This group of men were marked by prayer.

They were the reason we were seeing God do what He was doing at that time in the life of that church.

I joined them for a few of those Saturdays, but those were few and far between. Being marked by prayer was not on my radar at that time, and I regret not taking the time to learn from those men. Many, if not all, of them are no longer alive. I don't know if anyone else stepped up to continue the weekly praying. What I do know is their prayers made a difference in the life of that church, city, and individuals who were reached by that church in that season.

Imagine what might happen in your church if a few people were willing to be marked by prayer, to approach God with the hope of seeing Him reach a community or city for His glory regardless of whom God used or how He did it.

Imagine Sunday school classes ending their weekly gathering with a time of prayer that grew out of the passages studied during that hour, committing to follow God in whatever way He saw fit.

Imagine what God might do in a worship service that included a time of focused prayer based on the passages studied in the Bible study groups that met that day (or week).

Imagine what might happen if the people who attended the Bible study groups and worship then spent some of their prayer time during the week echoing the emphasis of the Bible passage studied, expressing their willingness to follow Jesus and His plans for them?

What keeps us—what keeps me—from carrying these marks? Why am I hesitant to embrace my helplessness? What keeps me from maintaining a discipline of studying and praying Scripture? What sins am I ignoring to avoid the grief they should produce in my heart? How does my ego get in the way of deferring to God? Why am I not consumed with being in the presence of God?

These challenging questions require an honest look into who we are and what we really trust and who we are really following. These questions and others made the writing of this book painful, challenging, and one of the most rewarding things I have done in several years.

Being marked by prayer takes time, effort, and transparency. We may have to admit hurts and reach out to people we have not seen in years to get things right. We may need to come to grips with our limits and mortality, embracing both. We may need to learn to remove ourselves from the top of the credits and let others, including God, get the credit they deserve. We may need to stop doing some activity, even a good one, so we can spend time in study and with the Father to get in sync with His heart. None of this is easy or painless. But then, anything worth doing is difficult and painful in some way.

We began this journey with me admitting that I felt inadequate to write this book, much less be a champion of prayer. Those feelings of inadequacy still exist, but that does not deter me from seeking to become a person marked by prayer. My understanding of prayer has changed over the years, seeing it more in terms of talking to the Father who has a plan for this world as opposed to a child who wants to improve his Father's plans. God continues to have a great deal to teach me about prayer. My hope is that you will join me in the quest of being marked by prayer. It will not be easy, but it will be worth it.

Onward.

NOTES

1. John 13:35, Benson Commentary, "By this shall all men know that you are my disciples," Bible.hub, accessed May 29, 2025, https://biblehub.com/commentaries/john/13-35.htm.

2. T. W. Hunt, *The Doctrine of Prayer* (Broadman & Holman Publishers, 1999), 15.

3. Olin Binkley, *How to Study the Bible* (Convention Press, 1969), 38–40.

4. For more on this, see *Building a Disciple-Making Ministry: The Timeless Principles of Arthur Flake for Sunday School and Small Groups* (Lifeway Christian Resources, 2020), 22.

5. This model has been used for centuries by many different Christian leaders and organizations. Some even believe it dates back to the early Church Fathers.

6. Claude King, *Return to Me* (Lifeway Press, 2020), 17.

7. Note: Also included in my previous work, *It Begins with Prayer: How Prayer Impacts Reaching Others, Building Community, and Serving Through the Sunday School* (Lifeway Christian Resources, 2019).

ABOUT THE AUTHOR

G. Dwayne McCrary is the manager of adult ongoing Bible studies at Lifeway and is also an adjunct professor at Midwestern Baptist Theological Seminary. He has degrees from Dallas Baptist University (BA), Southwestern Baptist Theological Seminary (MARE), and New Orleans Baptist Theological Seminary (DEdMin). Prior to coming to Lifeway, Dr. McCrary served on church staff for more than twenty plus years, mostly in Texas. On most Sundays, you will find him teaching an adult Bible study group, attending worship, and then teaching a preschool class. In his spare time, you can find him on a date with his wife of forty years, investing in his two kids and four grandkids, reading a history book, or on his road bicycle.